THE VALUE OF FANTASY

The Story of Hans Christian Andersen

VALUE COMMUNICATIONS, INC.
PUBLISHERS
LA JOLLA, CALIFORNIA

THE VALUE OF FANTASY

The Story of
Hans Christian Andersen

BY SPENCER JOHNSON, M.D.

THE DANBURY PRESS

The Value of Fantasy is part of the ValueTales series.

The Value of Fantasy text copyright © 1979 by Spencer Johnson, M.D. Illustrations copyright © 1979 by Value Communications, Inc.

First Edition
Manufactured in the United States of America
For information write to: ValueTales, P.O.Box 1012
La Jolla, CA 92038

Library of Congress Cataloging in Publication Data

Johnson, Spencer.
    The value of fantasy.

    (Value tales)
    SUMMARY: A brief biography of the 19th-century Danish author of many well-known fairy tales, which stresses the value of personal fantasies and imagination.
    1.   Andersen, Hans Christian, 1805-1875 — Biography — Juvenile literature. 2.   Authors, Danish — 19th century — Biography — Juvenile literature. [1.   Andersen, Hans Christian, 1805-1875. 2.   Authors, Danish.
3.   Imagination]   I.   Title. PT8119. J6
839.8'1'36 [B] [92]   79-18237

ISBN 0-916392-43-0

Dedicated to Lucky Roberts for all that he
has done

This tale is about a person who shared his
fantasies with the world, Hans Christian
Andersen. The story that follows is based on
events in his life. More historical facts about Hans
Christian Andersen can be found on page 63.

6

Once upon a time...

long, long ago, in the tiny village of Odense in Denmark, there lived a boy named Hans Christian Andersen.

Hans Christian was a poor boy. More often than not, he ran about with patches on his sleeves and wooden shoes on his bare feet. But in spite of the patches and the wooden shoes—and the fact that sometimes he went to bed hungry—Hans was happy. His mother loved him dearly, and she kept the little cottage where the Andersens lived clean and shining.

Hans Christian's father was a shoemaker who worked long hours and made little money. But in the evenings that didn't seem to matter. In the evenings he read to Hans—marvelous tales about elves and sprites and emperors and princesses.

Shoemaker Andersen made toys for Hans, too. The most wonderful one was a tiny theater where puppets appeared in little plays that Hans made up himself.

Hans was usually the only audience at the puppet plays. He didn't have many friends. He was so busy making up fantastic stories in his head that sometimes he didn't even hear what people said to him.

Hans was homely, too—skinny and awkward and too tall for his age. The other children made fun of him.

"Never mind," Hans would say whenever this happened. "When I am grown up, I will be rich and famous. I will live in a palace and will have tea everyday with the Emperor of China."

Then Hans would creep into the secret place under the gooseberry bush where he had made a little tent with his mother's apron and a broomstick. He would close his eyes and imagine how grand it would be to have tea with the emperor, to live in a palace and eat little chocolate cakes and wear silk clothes and slippers with great tassels on them.

9

"Sometimes I worry about Hans," said his mother to the women of the village. "He will never be satisfied with an ordinary trade. He always wants to do something grand. Do you know that he wants to build a castle right here in our village? Every night he sits and makes plans for his castle."

"Do not be afraid," said one of the women. She was very old and rather strange. "He will be a wild bird, flying high. He will be admired by all the world, and some day our village will be decked with lights because of him."

The old lady never explained this prophecy, but Hans's mother thought of it often as her son sat with his puppet theater and made up plays for his little dolls. She thought of it, too, when she took Hans to the country for the hop-picking. He listened to the peasants tell the old folktales of Denmark, and when he came home he could repeat every one of the stories to his father.

"They may be true stories," said Fru Andersen, who was quite superstitious. "Just the same, I wish Hans would spend more time studying and less time thinking about such things. He might learn a steady trade. He could be a shoemaker like you, or perhaps a tailor."

"Never!" cried her husband. "Hans will do better things than to make shoes or cut coats for other people." And Hans's father began to read to him from the *Arabian Nights.*

It was about this time that Hans learned a very interesting thing. According to the schoolmaster, China was on the far side of the earth, exactly opposite Denmark. If a Dane dug a hole deep enough, he would come out in Peking or Shanghai or some other exotic city.

"But if we can dig our way to China," said Hans to himself, "why shouldn't the Chinese dig their way to Denmark? Perhaps one will. Perhaps a prince will come, and he will help me to build my beautiful castle!"

Now Hans saw no reason this fantastic thing shouldn't happen. And the longer he thought about it, the more he believed that it might be happening at that very moment.

"If the prince *is* coming," said he, "he is surely coming through the river. That's the lowest place in town, so it's the nearest to China. If I go to the river and sing a beautiful song, the prince will hear it and he'll dig faster to find out who the singer is."

And Hans took himself and his wooden shoes and his patches and tatters to the river and began to sing for the prince who was digging his way through the earth from China.

13

Hans sang and sang, for he had a pleasant voice and he loved to use it. But no matter how sweetly he sang, no prince came out of the water. Instead, a mother duck paddled to the shore with her five ducklings behind her. She waddled up onto the riverbank, smoothed her feathers, then began to lead her babies away.

The last one to scramble out of the river was an ugly little duckling with short legs, feet that were too big for the rest of him, and a bill that was too broad. His feathers didn't lie flat, but ruffled themselves every which way so that he looked more like a walking feather duster than a duckling.

The mother quacked at the ugly little one, and it was an impatient, scolding sort of quack. Then the other ducklings ran ahead of him, leaving him to hurry along on his big feet as best he could.

14

"Never mind," said Hans to the duckling. "Perhaps you're not a duck at all. Perhaps you're a changeling. The fairies took you from your real mother one night, and when you're grown everyone will see that you're truly a beautiful swan."

When Hans said this, a very strange thing happened.

15

The little duck vanished for a moment into the tall reeds at the edge of the river. Then he waddled out again and looked up at Hans in a questioning way.

"Things aren't always what they seem," said Hans. "For instance, you may think that I'm only singing to myself here beside the river. In truth, I'm singing to the Chinese prince. Right now the prince is busy digging his way from China, and he needs to be encouraged."

The duck quacked in an odd way, very much as if he were laughing at Hans. Then he said, "If a Chinese prince—or any other prince—comes out of that river, I'm a prince, too! I'm Hamlet, Prince of Denmark!"

"Why shouldn't you be Hamlet, Prince of Denmark, if you like?" asked Hans. "Hamlet is a very nice name for a duck."

"Call me whatever you want to," said the duckling. "It's all the same to me. I'm not real, you know. I'm just another of your fantasies. Ducks simply do not talk with people."

"They talk with me," said Hans Christian Andersen. Then he picked the ugly duckling up and carried him home under his arm.

17

"Very nice," said Hamlet when he saw the snug room where Hans lived with his mother and father. Indeed it was nice, for Fru Andersen had hung some colored pictures on the walls, and there was a shelf in the corner where plates and cups and mugs gleamed in the firelight.

"I think I'll like it here," said Hamlet when Fru Andersen pulled down the little bench where Hans slept at night. It would be cozy to lie there, separated from the rest of the room by a curtain, and to dream wonderful dreams.

Fru Andersen didn't object when Hans took the ugly duckling to bed with him, for Fru Andersen couldn't see Hamlet. She only knew that Hans seemed happier than usual. And Hans *was* happy, for he had a friend—someone who could whisper with him about his fantasies.

"I will tell you a secret," said Hans to Hamlet. "Someday I will be famous. One of the old women in the town told my mother, and you know how old women are. They *know* things!"

"What will you do to become famous?" asked Hamlet.

Hans thought for a moment and then he decided. "I will be an actor and perform on the stage, and everyone will clap for me!"

Not long after Hans met Hamlet, tragedy came to the little cottage in that humble street in Odense. Hans's father fell sick and died.

"What will you do now?" said the neighbors to Fru Andersen. They looked at Hans in a way that made the boy anxious and afraid.

"You have no money," one of them told Fru Andersen.

Hans's mother knew this quite well. She didn't need to be reminded. "I will take in laundry," she said bravely.

"The boy can help," said the woman. "Look! He is eleven years old, and a fine, tall lad. Let him go to the cloth factory and work there!"

"I don't know how they can call you a fine, tall lad," said Hamlet the duck. "You're a gawky boy, that's what you are, with your shoes too big for you and your elbows out of your sleeves. And if you go to work in the cloth factory, how will you ever become an actor?"

"I'll practice," Hans decided. "I'll sing for the foreman and the other workers, and I'll recite. They'll enjoy my performances. You'll see!"

21

"I hope this works out all right," said Hamlet, "but I have a feeling it may not."

"You worry too much," Hans declared. "I'm going to be a famous actor. The old woman said so."

And Hans took himself off to the cloth factory with his bread and cheese for lunch tied up in a kerchief.

22

"It isn't someday I'm worried about," said Hamlet as he waddled after Hans. "It's right now."

When they reached the cloth factory, Hamlet perched on one of the great looms and watched Hans begin his career.

First Hans sang for the foreman and the other boys who worked in the factory. Then he recited. He waved his arms and shouted at the exciting parts. The men listened patiently for a little while, but then they began to make fun of Hans and to imitate him. They waved their arms, and they cried out that Hans looked exactly like a windmill—a broken windmill!

"I was afraid of this," said Hamlet. "The world isn't ready for Hans yet—or perhaps Hans isn't ready for the world."

Hans went home that night with tears running down his face.

"It's all right, Hans," said his mother when she saw the boy come down the street with his head bowed and his shoulders hunched as if he were cold. "You don't need to go back there again with those rough fellows."

The neighbor women agreed that the crew at the cloth factory were anything but polite. "But what about the snuff factory?" said one. "Making snuff is nice work, and not too difficult."

So it was decided that Hans would try his luck at the snuff factory.

"I think this time I won't recite for the men," he told Hamlet. "I'll just do as I'm told."

"I think that would be a fine idea," agreed Hamlet. "The people who own the factory will probably be just as happy if you don't sing, either."

25

Hans tried to be bright and industrious at the snuff factory. He
hardly performed at all. However, he did let his mind wander. He
paid more attention to the fantasies he made up in his head—to
the witches and princes and mermaids—than he did to making snuff.

"Here you! Andersen!" shouted the foreman. "Watch what you're doing!"

Hans jumped and he sneezed. So did Hamlet sneeze. Who could
help sneezing in such a place? The air was filled with snuff, which
is nothing more or less than powdered tobacco.

Hans was still sneezing when he went home that evening, and his eyes were red and watery.

"You're sick!" said his mother. She looked at his throat to see if it was red, which it was. She felt his forehead to see if it was warm.

"It's only the snuff that makes me sneeze, Mother," said Hans.

"Oh dear!" said his mother. "It's bad for your lungs. You mustn't go back there, Hans. It could be the death of you!"

27

Hans did not go back to the snuff factory. It wasn't his lungs he was worried about, but his voice. If he was to be an actor, he had to take care of his voice.

And so Hans stayed at home in the little cottage. When he could, he recited for the ladies of the village. They gave him pocket money and lent him books.

Once—just once—Hans went to the theater. He was so thrilled by the play—the lights, the crowds, the excitement, and the applause—that he could hardly sleep for weeks afterward. He spent more and more time with his puppet theater, and he made up wonderful dramas for his puppets to act.

"Very nice, I'm sure," said Hamlet the duck, "but are you going to spend your life playing with puppets?"

"Indeed I'm not," said Hans. "The moment I'm old enough, I'm going to Copenhagen. I won't come back to Odense until I'm rich and famous. Then I'll ride into town in the coach and get out at the inn wearing elegant clothes, and everyone will whisper, 'There goes Hans Christian, the Widow Andersen's son!'"

But the Widow Andersen did not remain the Widow Andersen forever. When Hans was thirteen, his mother married again. Hans's stepfather was a shoemaker, just as Hans's father had been.

"He's a pleasant enough fellow," said Hamlet the duck, when the new husband moved into the cottage where once Hans's father had worked. "He seems very fond of your mother."

It was true enough, but it made Hans feel strange to see this man sitting at his father's bench, and calling his mother "Wife." And the stepfather never read to Hans in the evenings.

"I think he will not miss me if I go away," said Hans to Hamlet. "I think it is time for me to start my career in Copenhagen."

And when he was barely fourteen, Hans Christian Andersen shook out of his bank all the bits of money he had saved over the years, and he set out for the great city.

The coach to Copenhagen bumped and jounced across the countryside, through great and small towns. Then it clattered aboard the ferry that crossed the stretch of water called the Great Belt.

Hans stood at the rail as the ferry pulled away from shore, and he looked at the wild waves. "Just think, Hamlet," said he. "There is probably another kingdom down there, beneath the water. Can't you just see the towers and the castles and the palaces? The mermaids swim through the streets, and they bow nicely to one another as they pass. And perhaps, if we watch closely, we'll see one come to the surface and peep about."

"If any do come to the surface, they won't find me there!" said Hamlet. "That's entirely too much water for a duck who was raised in a river!"

After what seemed an age, the ferry came to shore. Then the coach jounced and bumped on again, and passed through still more great towns and small ones. And at last, when it seemed to Hans and Hamlet that they had been journeying since the beginning of the world, a cry went up from the driver.

"There it is!" he shouted.

Do you know what he had seen?

He had seen the towers of Copenhagen off in the distance.

"All right, Andersen," he said to the boy. "This is as far as I can take you. You'll have to walk the rest of the way."

Hans got down from the coach quite willingly, but Hamlet quacked an angry quack. "What's the matter?" demanded the duck. "Nobody else is getting out of the coach here. Why can't we ride on into the city?"

"Because I didn't have enough money to pay the full fare to Copenhagen," said Hans. "The driver said he'd take me only if I got off outside the town, so the officials wouldn't know he'd let me ride for lower fare."

"Oh dear!" groaned poor Hamlet as the coach rolled away. "It looks like such a long walk to Copenhagen. And I'm such a short-legged duck!"

"No problem!" said Hans with a laugh. Then he tucked the duck into his satchel and strode on. And so Hamlet came into Copenhagen very comfortably, with his head poking out of Hans's bag and his feet curled up cozy as could be in Hans's second-best shirt.

"My word!" said Hamlet as Hans carried him through the streets of the great city. "Look at all the people! There must be thousands and thousands—and they all talk at once!"

Hans grinned. "Soon they'll be talking about me!" he predicted. "Wait and see!"

"You're a modest fellow, you are," said Hamlet.

"The old woman said I'd be famous," said Hans. "I'll be auditioned for a part in the theater, and of course I'll be accepted."

And Hans hurried to the house where the director of the Royal Theater lived.

"I have a feeling this will be even bumpier than the stagecoach ride," said Hamlet in a gloomy voice.

"Have faith!" cried Hans. "How can I fail? It's my destiny to be great!"

With that, Hans rang the doorbell.

And what do you suppose happened?

A pretty little maid opened the door. She was startled to see a tall, tow-headed boy there with a rumpled coat and patched breeches. But there was something about Hans that she liked, so she ran to tell the director that he had a caller.

Hans was invited in, and he was treated very kindly. The director listened to him recite, and he frowned when Hans waved his arms. Then he smiled when Hans sang a little song for him, and he agreed that Hans was rather graceful when Hans danced a step or two.

38

"My goodness!" said Hamlet. "Maybe Hans Christian's fantasies aren't as fantastic as I thought."

When Hans had displayed all of his accomplishments, the director looked very serious. "You have a sweet voice," he said. "I'm afraid I can't say much for your other talents. Why don't you go to see Siboni? He's the Italian who directs the Royal Singing Academy. He may find a place for you."

"Being a singer is almost as good as being an actor," said Hamlet. "You can be just as famous!"

"Indeed I can!" shouted Hans, and he thanked the director most warmly. Then he ran all the way to the house of Signor Siboni.

The Italian musician was having a banquet when Hans arrived. Hans did not let this stop him for an instant. He stood up bravely before all the guests, and he sang for the splendid gentlemen and the beautiful ladies who gleamed with satin and sparkled with jewels.

"How quaint!" said the ladies. One of them looked at Hans through her eyeglasses as if he were a creature from another world entirely.

"The boy is sincere, and his voice is not bad," said Siboni. "Perhaps I can use him."

The great man smiled at Hans. "I have a feeling, young fellow, that you're not very wealthy," he said.

Hans looked down at his faded, mended clothes, and he blushed. "I have no money at all," he said.

"We shall see what we can do about that," said one of the guests. He was a kindly composer named Weyse, and he took up a collection for Hans on the spot.

"Perhaps that old woman in Odense really knew what she was talking about," said Hamlet the duck. "Siboni is going to teach Hans, and he has a little money to keep him until he becomes famous!"

But before six months had passed, a dreadful misfortune overtook Hans. He began to lose his voice.

"My poor boy," said Siboni. "It's a pity, but there is nothing anyone can do. It happens sometimes that the voice does not last. You will have to find something else to do."

Hans trudged away with a heavy heart.

"Something else to do," said Hans sadly. "What could it be? The director of the Royal Theater says I cannot be an actor. I am too tall to be a dancer . . ."

"And too awkward," said Hamlet, but he did not say it unkindly. "Perhaps you should give up this fantasy of being famous," he said. "Why not go back to Odense and become an apprentice—and have a trade like your father?"

Do you think that's what Hans did?

Surely not! "When I go home, I will go like a prince!" he said, and for the next three years he and Hamlet drifted about in Copenhagen. They lived in miserable little rooms up many flights of stairs. Hans put papers in his shoes to keep the rain out, and he wore the clothes that kind friends gave him.

"That's much too short for you," said Hamlet one day, when Hans put on an old vest that he liked especially well.

"No one will notice if I don't stand straight," declared Hans. He hunched his shoulders so as to seem shorter, and he went off to find some odd jobs he could do. Sometimes he recited for the guests at the great houses, and sometimes he was allowed to be in a crowd scene at the Royal Theater.

"This is an awful way to make a living," Hamlet complained. "Anything would be better. Your father was a good, respectable shoemaker, and . . ."

"And he hated being a good respectable shoemaker!" Hans cried. "He wanted me to do better, and I *will* do better. If I can't be an actor or a singer, I'll be a poet!"

And Hans began to write. He composed wonderful, thundering plays and romantic dramas and high-flown, sentimental poems.

Soon he had a heap of manuscripts which he carried with him everywhere.

"Fascinating!" said Hamlet, poking his bill through the stacks of scribbled paper. "You realize, of course, that you don't know how to spell, let alone write."

"Spelling is a mere detail," said Hans Christian Andersen, who refused to let himself be discouraged.

Just the same, Hans suspected that a proper writer *would* know how to spell, so he didn't often allow anyone to read his manuscripts. Instead, Hans recited the plays and the poems to the actors and directors at the theater. Most of them listened patiently.

"You see?" said Hans to Hamlet. "They like what I write. It won't be any time before I have a play presented on the stage."

"Poor Hans," said Hamlet sadly. "Can't you tell? They are sorry for you. They're simply being polite!"

Hans knew that Hamlet was probably right. After all, the duck was truly Hans's own better judgment. Just the same, when he was seventeen, Hans submitted two plays to the Royal Theater. Of course the directors did not produce the plays, but one of the directors—a man named Jonas Collin—decided that Hans should have a grant from the king so that he could go to school.

"You must have some education," Collin told Hans. "If you go on as you are, idling about the streets, making up wild adventures, reciting for pennies at the homes of the wealthy people of the town, you will fall into some terrible trouble."

"You mean I am to have a chance?" cried Hans. He felt his heart give a great thump. "I am to go to school? Then I will really be a poet!"

"Just a moment, young man!" said Jonas Collin. He looked severely at Hans. "I believe that you can make something of yourself, but you must pay attention. You must stop scribbling plays and poems, and you must study hard. Promise that you will not try to write even a single little fairy tale while you are at school."

Hans was terribly disappointed, but he wanted very much to go to school. He promised he would not write any more stories, at least for the time being.

Off went Hans to a town called Slagelse, where he attended classes at the grammar school and made his home with the headmaster, a man named Meisling.

Meisling had no patience at all with Hans. He saw that the boy's mind wasn't disciplined. Hans could remember fascinating bits of history, and he could recite long, romantic poems. However, he had trouble with grammar, and it seemed that no matter how he tried, he would never learn to spell.

50

"You are a dolt and an idiot!" scolded Headmaster Meisling. "You will wind up in the gutter if you don't improve—or in the madhouse!"

"Don't pay any attention to him," Hamlet whispered. "He may know all the Latin verbs and the Greek classics, but he has dirty fingernails and he hasn't bathed in a month. Also, in case you haven't noticed, he isn't a good teacher. He doesn't like any of his students—and they don't like him!"

"But what if he is right!" Hans cried. "Suppose I *do* wind up in the gutter? Or the madhouse?"

"You won't," said Hamlet in his practical way. "Pay attention and do your work and you will be fine. Now you need a little rest, so go and play with the children."

Hans always took heart when Hamlet spoke that way, and he did as Hamlet suggested. He went into the parlor where Headmaster Meisling's children were waiting for him. He watched over the children and played games with them. That wasn't a bit strange; Hans was hardly more than a child himself.

Hans never broke his promise to Jonas Collin. He didn't write any more plays or poems while he was in school. But he had never promised that he wouldn't tell tales to children, and the Meisling youngsters loved his stories. They ran to him whenever he appeared in the parlor and begged him to make up more wonderful adventures for them.

''I think this is the thing about school that I like best,'' said Hamlet—for the ugly little duckling liked the stories, too. He always stayed close when Hans talked about enchanted castles and magic kingdoms and valiant tin soldiers and talking frogs and princesses and match girls and owls and nightingales.

Hans never became a brilliant student. His head was so crammed with fantasy that there was little room for anything else. But he did at last learn to discipline his thoughts and at last he went to the university in Copenhagen.

"I am so grateful for all that you have done," he said to Jonas Collin, when he finished at the university. "And now I can begin to write again."

Collin sighed. "You must do what you want with your own life," he said, "but I had hoped you would choose something more practical."

Hamlet the duck sighed a bit, too. "You still don't spell very well," he reminded Hans. "You will never write Latin prose as the elegant gentlemen do. Are you sure you don't want to forget about poetry and use your education by becoming a clerk in some government office?"

"You know better than that!" cried Hans, and he set to work with his paper and pen. Soon he had written a poem called "The Dying Child." It wasn't classical or elegant, but it was sincere. Hans had written it with great feeling.

"Not too bad," said Hamlet. "Perhaps you could even get it published."

55

Hamlet was right. Hans's poem was published, and people began to say nice things about the poor young man from Odense. This gave Hans new courage. He began to write his inmost thoughts and fantasies. More and more of his work was published, and he was given another grant from the king so that he did not need to be so anxious about money.

But Hans was accustomed to being anxious, and to worrying about himself. At times he still brooded about his fate and wondered what would finally become of him.

Hamlet always became quite brisk when he saw that this was happening. "Time to go on a journey, Hans," he would say. "Come along. Pack your bag. You're taking yourself much too seriously. You need new things to think about."

56

Hans would pack then, and take his big traveling umbrella. Off he would go by train or steamship to such places as Holland and Italy and Turkey and Greece. Hamlet went along, of course. Hamlet went everywhere with Hans. And when they were on a ship, the duckling perched on the rail and looked out over the waves and remembered how it was when he and Hans rode the ferry across the stretch of water called the Great Belt, and how they imagined the mermaids playing under the waves.

After he had been writing plays and poetry and sketches for several years, and after he had traveled all over Europe, Hans brought out a novel called *The Improvisator*. It was really a disguised version of Hans's life, and it was a great success. People flocked to the bookshops to buy it.

"Wonderful, isn't it?" said Hans to Hamlet. "My fantasies have come true. I am famous, and here I sit in my slippers and my silk robe, with the stove making cozy sounds at me. I am still an ugly duckling like you, with a big nose and a small chin, but I am very happy."

"Not all ugly ducklings become swans," said Hamlet, "and it *is* nice to live this way. And since your fantasies for yourself have come true, what about those other fantasies?"

Hamlet scrambled up to sit beside Hans on the sofa. "Remember the children in old man Meisling's parlor?" he said. "Remember all the children who have listened to your stories? Didn't you have fun telling fairy tales to those children? And is it possible that your fairy tales are more true than your stylish novel? They are about strength and love and goodness and life and hope, aren't they?"

Hamlet looked squarely at Hans. "I will tell you a secret, Hans Christian Andersen," he said. "I like your fairy tales better than your novel—and I think perhaps you do, too."

It was true and Hans Christian knew it. Quickly he set to work to write down those other fantasies. He retold the story of the princess who could not sleep on a pea, and of the emperor who wanted new clothes. He wrote of the little mermaid who fell in love with a mortal, and of the nightingale who sang for the Emperor of China.

Hans wrote of the Snow Queen, too, and told how she stole away the boy named Kay. He wrote of the little match girl and the wild swans, the steadfast tin soldier and the maiden who danced away in her red shoes.

What happened when Hans Christian Andersen published these fantasies? They were not elegant or stylish. They were simple children's tales. But everyone loved them, and everyone clamored for more and more—and still more.

Once the fairy tales began to appear, Hans was truly famous with a fame that would never dwindle. He was invited to speak to groups of authors. When he went to England, he stayed with the great writer, Charles Dickens. And all his life long he dined with emperors and kings, as he had once dreamed he would. His name is still the proudest in all of proud Copenhagen, and, as the old woman foretold, Odense was lighted in his honor. People know it today as the town where he was born.

61

Perhaps there are times when you have fantasies, too—when you tell yourself stories and dream dreams. Your fantasies may not be about kings and princesses or mermaids and nightingales. They can be quite different. And you may not even wish to be famous. But if you decide to make room in your life for some dreams, whatever they may be—to take a little time for fantasy—you may find that you are happier.

Just like our good friend Hans Christian Andersen.

The End

Hans Christian Andersen was born in 1805 to a desperately poor couple who lived in a one-room cottage in the slums of Odense, in Denmark. His father was a shoemaker who had dreamed of a greater career for himself. It is possible that some of those dreams inspired Hans. His mother was uneducated and superstitious, but she loved her son dearly, and he remembered her always with tremendous affection.

Hans's father died in 1816, and some attempts were made to put the boy to work. These came to nothing. Fru Anderson did not want her son exposed to the company of rough laboring men. The poor widow became a laundress to support herself and Hans, and two years after her husband's death she married again.

Hans went to Copenhagen when he was in his teens. He was determined to win fame as a singer, a dancer, or an actor. He was a complete failure at all of these professions and was reduced almost to begging. Although he lived in grinding poverty, Hans was never corrupted. He remained innocent, and he kept the ability to charm important, talented people with his earnestness and enthusiasm.

There is no doubt that Hans was stagestruck. He remained close to the Royal Theater all during his difficult teen years, and having failed as a performer, he tried to become a dramatist. The boy had almost no formal education, however, and in 1822, with the help of Jonas Collin, a director of the theater, Hans received a grant so that he could enter school at Slagelse.

Hans's school years were not happy, since the headmaster at Slagelse was a bully and a brute. In 1827, Collin took the boy away from the school and arranged for private tutors. Soon Hans went on to complete his education at Copenhagen University.

His writing career began in earnest in 1827 with the publication of the poem "The Dying Child." Other poems followed, as well as plays and sketches—most especially travel sketches. He loved to travel, and was always stimulated and refreshed by his journeys.

In 1835, Hans Christian wrote *The Improvisator*, a novel that was very popular. Hans was

HANS CHRISTIAN ANDERSEN
1805–1875

tremendously pleased with his novel, and perhaps not so hopeful about the fate of the fairy tales. The first of these were also published in 1835. Today the fairy tales are read in every corner of the world, and there are few people outside Denmark who have ever heard of *The Improvisator*.

All of his life Andersen was a difficult, complex character. He was vain, sensitive to criticism, and bedeviled by his own moods. However, he was also capable of deep and lasting affection and gratitude, and there were several occasions on which he generously forgave people who had wounded him deeply. Few writers have been feted as he was, and he gloried in receiving the attention, yet there always remained in him a bit of the gawky boy who came to the great city with his elbows sticking out of his sleeves.

He died in 1875, after writing and rewriting his memoirs and announcing happily that his life had been a beautiful fairy tale. This may be another fantasy, one of the thousands that sustained Andersen during his youth and comforted him in later years. If one doubts Andersen himself, however, one cannot disbelieve a statement made by his friend Edvard Collin, son of Hans's patron, Jonas Collin. Collin wrote a book that is not entirely free of criticism of Andersen. But Collin has this to say of the famous writer: "I have looked into the depths of his soul . . . I know that he was good."

Other Titles in the ValueTale Series